Theory Paper   Grade 2   2014   A
Model Answers

1 (10)

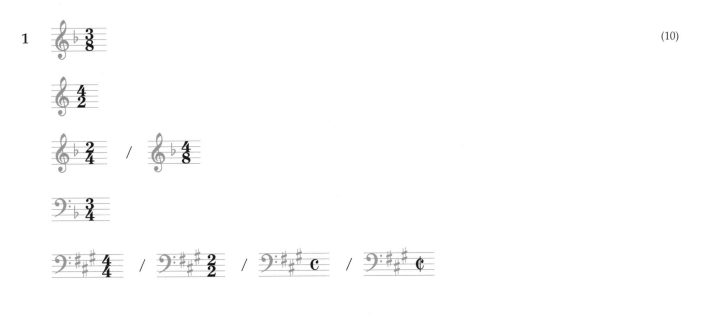

2 *There are many ways of completing this question. The specimen completion below would receive full marks.* (10)

3   G major   A minor   D major   (10)

   Eb major   D minor

4 (10)

5 (10)

6 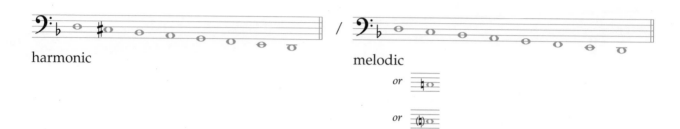 (10)

harmonic   melodic

or ♮○

or (♮)○

7   (10)

(a)   4th   6th   3rd   1st /   2nd   4th   5th   7th   8th /
                                8th / 8ve   8ve / 1st

(b)

8   (a)   with movement / with motion / moving   (10)
              moderately loud / half loud / medium loud
              play the notes smoothly / slur
              getting louder / gradually getting louder
              accent / forced / accented

(b)   (10)

(i)

(ii)   four
(iii) 6

(iv)

(v)   C

(c)    (10)

Grade

2

Music Theory
Past Papers
2014

Model Answers

ABRSM Grade 2

Welcome to ABRSM's *Music Theory Past Papers 2014 Model Answers*, Grade 2. These answers are a useful resource for students and teachers preparing for ABRSM theory exams and should be used alongside the relevant published theory past papers.

All the answers in this booklet would receive full marks but not all possible answers have been included for practicable reasons. In these cases other reasonable alternatives may also be awarded full marks. For composition-style questions (where candidates must complete a rhythm, compose a melody based on a given opening or set text to music) only one example of the many possible answers is given.

For more information on how theory papers are marked and some general advice on taking theory exams, please refer to the Music Theory Grade 2 web page: www.abrsm.org/theory2.

Using these answers

- Answers are given in the same order and, where possible, in the same layout as in the exam papers, making it easy to match answer to question.

- Where it is necessary to show the answer on a stave, the original stave is printed in grey with the answer shown in black, for example:

- Alternative answers are separated by an oblique stroke (/) or by *or*, for example:

getting slower / gradually getting slower

- The old-style crotchet rest 𝄽 is accepted as a valid alternative to the modern symbol 𝄽 .

- Answers that require the candidate to write out a scale or chord have been shown at one octave only. Reasonable alternatives at different octaves can also receive full marks.

- Sometimes the clef, key and time signature of the relevant bar(s) are included for added clarity, for example:

© 2015 by The Associated Board of the Royal Schools of Music
Published by ABRSM (Publishing) Ltd, a wholly owned subsidiary of ABRSM
Cover by Kate Benjamin & Andy Potts
Printed in England by Page Bros (Norwich) Ltd

Theory Paper   Grade 2   2014   B
Model Answers

1   (10)

2   *There are many ways of completing this question. The specimen completion below would receive full marks.*   (10)

3   (10)

(a)

(b)   D major

4   (10)

harmonic   *or*   /   melodic

          or

5   6th   4th   2nd   (10)
          3rd   8th / 8ve   5th

6 (10)

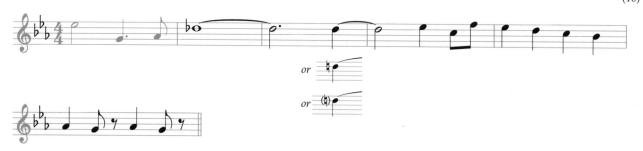

7 (10)

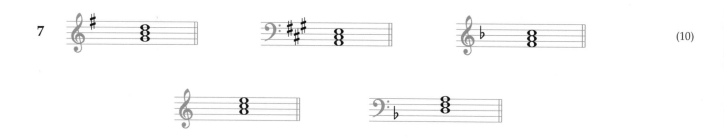

8 (a) (10)

slow / at ease / leisurely
much / very
sustained
the number of beats in a bar / two beats in a bar
quiet / soft

(b) (10)

    (i)   5
    (ii)   5th
    (iii)   quaver / eighth note
    (iv)   6 ; 7
    (v)   *legato* (smoothly)

Adagio molto sostenuto

(c)  (10)

Theory Paper   Grade 2   2014   C
Model Answers

1 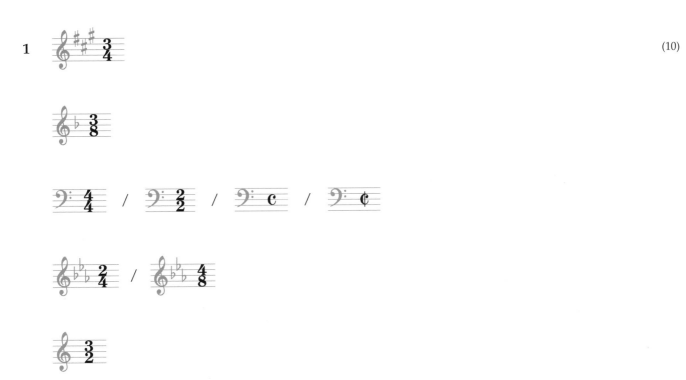 (10)

2 *There are many ways of completing this question. The specimen completion below would receive full marks.* (10)

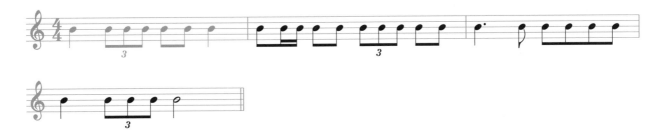

3 (10)

4 (10)

(a)   A   F♯   B   G   E   C♯   A   D   F♯

(b)   two / two quavers / two eighth notes / one crotchet / one quarter note / one beat

5  (10)

6  (10)

7  (10)

8 (a) at a walking pace / medium speed (10)
expressive / expressively / with expression
play the notes smoothly / slur
getting quieter / gradually getting quieter
very quiet / very soft

(b) (10)
    (i)   3rd
    (ii)   F major
    (iii) true
    (iv) *There are seven possible answers to this question. Any of the answers shown would receive full marks.*

    (v)   12

(c)  (10)

Music Theory Past Papers 2014 Model Answers

Model answers for four past papers from ABRSM's 2014 Theory exams for Grade 2

Key features:

- a list of correct answers where appropriate
- a selection of likely options where the answer can be expressed in a variety of ways
- a single exemplar where a composition-style answer is required

Support material for ABRSM Theory exams

ABRSM
24 Portland Place
London W1B 1LU
United Kingdom

www.abrsm.org

ABRSM is the exam board of the Royal Schools of M[...]
committed to actively supporting high-quality mus[...]
learning and development throughout the world, a[...]
the best possible resources for music teachers an[...]

£2.75   0615

ISBN 978-1-84849-713-9

9 781848 497139